The
YOUNG
and the
RESTED

The Young and the Rested

Alexsis Boles

XULON PRESS

Xulon Press
2301 Lucien Way #415
Maitland, FL 32751
407.339.4217
www.xulonpress.com

© 2022 by Alexsis Boles

All rights reserved solely by the author. The author guarantees all contents are original and do not infringe upon the legal rights of any other person or work. No part of this book may be reproduced in any form without the permission of the author.

Due to the changing nature of the Internet, if there are any web addresses, links, or URLs included in this manuscript, these may have been altered and may no longer be accessible. The views and opinions shared in this book belong solely to the author and do not necessarily reflect those of the publisher. The publisher therefore disclaims responsibility for the views or opinions expressed within the work.

Unless otherwise indicated, Scripture quotations taken from the New King James Version (NKJV). Copyright © 1982 by Thomas Nelson, Inc. Used by permission. All rights reserved.

Paperback ISBN-13: 978-1-66284-375-4
Ebook ISBN-13: 978-1-66284-376-1

Dedication

I dedicate this book to all those dealing with the spirits of depression and bipolar disorder. Know that there is a way out! Don't give up on yourself or your family!

God loves you, and He will see you through.

Table of Contents

Dedication v
Acknowledgments ix
Introduction xi

THE EXPERIENCES: THE EPISODES OF MY LIFE 1
Chapter 1:   It Happened 3
Chapter 2:   Stole 11
Chapter 3:   Square One 17
Chapter 4:   Rams in the Bush 23
Chapter 5:   The Pivotal Point 29
Chapter 6:   Unexpected Revival Visitors 35
Chapter 7:   The Power of Prayer 39
Chapter 8:   The Funeral 45
Chapter 9:   Not My Sister, Too 49
Chapter 10: You are Bipolar 53
Chapter 11: Denial 57
Chapter 12: Surprises 61

THE ENCOURAGEMENT 67
Chapter 13: Spiritual Dehydration 69
Chapter 14: Yes, You Can 73

The Exaltation..79
Chapter 15: Glory Belongs to Him.....................81

About the Author...83

Acknowledgments

God, without You, I could not have pushed past the painful memories I went through during that twelve-year period to get this book written and published. It was long and hard, but You stuck by me the entire time. I am forever grateful for all that You have done and are still doing for me. Thank You!

Thank you to my mother, Marie S. Rivers, and stepfather, Wille J. Rivers, Sr., for being there every step of the way by helping Reggie, the boys, and me.

To my siblings: Marcus, Rivka, and Nachella; thank you for all the nights you stayed up to make sure I was all right. I am forever grateful.

I thank my in-laws for your support when things became chaotic for Reggie, the boys, and me.

I thank my children, Javin and Rj, who didn't understand what was going on at the time but still loved me unconditionally.

I thank my dearest husband, Reggie, for doing all you knew to do at the time to get me the help I needed to bring normalcy back to our home. Most importantly, you have consistently honored your wedding vows to me for over twenty years. Reggie, you are a man of integrity and because of that I love you more than you will ever know.

Lastly, I thank everyone at Xulon Press. Thank you to my friend, Ingrid McKinley, for being obedient to the voice of God when He told you to tell me, "Write the book!"

God bless you all for everything you did to help me when my life was falling apart. I love you all! I couldn't have asked for a better support system.

Introduction

SOMETIMES, YOUNG PEOPLE are thought to have endless energy, but in reality, they also get tired of everyday life routines. Because of expectations from others, they keep pressing and don't stop to take time for themselves. The devil notices that and oppresses them to prevent them from focusing or resting mentally. Once he has distracted them, he torments them and has them thinking the stress, anxiety, and hopelessness are normal.

The enemy had me entangled with his thoughts about me for twelve years. He told me I was bipolar because it ran in my family. I couldn't completely accept it as being just an illness during those years, but I knew something strange was going on with me. At one point, I was medicated regularly and still had these "episodes" of racing thoughts and no self-control. So, I knew it had to be something other than a chemical imbalance; it was a spirit, perhaps legions of them.

In hindsight, I know I opened a door for this evil spirit to come in and torment me with words I had spoken to myself. I thank God for never leaving me, and my family for never shunning me. I am grateful for being among the "young and the rested," from the evil works of the enemy.

In the pages following, you will begin to read about the "episodes" of my life.

The Experiences: the Episodes of My Life

Chapter 1

IT HAPPENED

My buddy, my pea-in-the-pod, my ace boon-coon, my brother and I, decided we were going to join the U.S. Army National Guard in the summer of 1994. The day came to take the ASVAB test. The recruiter picked us up, and it seemed like the longest twenty-five-mile ride ever -- a ride we had taken many times before. While we were testing, I gave it my all by reading every question carefully and answering them to the best of my knowledge. On the other hand, my brother later revealed that he had just bubbled in random answers without reading the questions. Needless to say, he failed miserably. Well, when my test results came back, it looked like I was joining the U.S. Army National Guard alone, even though I was having second thoughts. My test results turned out decent, but I didn't expect to hear that I couldn't be a cook. I told the recruiter, "The test isn't accurate because I have great cooking skills!"

As time passed, my brother was doing his own thing, and I was trying hard to prepare myself for boot camp to become a soldier. I had people doing their best to talk me out of it, but it had been a year since I'd been out of college, and the probability of me going back was slim to none. I didn't want to be a burden to my single-parent mother, who was working a minimum wage ($4.25/hour) job. My mother was also raising my two younger siblings. So, I just ignored everyone's attempts to get me to back out because my focus was to help my mother by taking care of myself.

I enlisted.

On February 13th, 1995 (the night before boot camp), I was lying down on the sofa, wondering what I had gotten myself into? Two months prior, when I was at guard duty, I remembered a young female soldier telling me that I would be in a foxhole with live grenades being thrown at me. As you can probably imagine, that didn't sit so well with me since I was already having second thoughts. I knew I was in way over my head, but I was stuck, and there was no way out; I belonged to Uncle Sam. I had already been sworn in to be a soldier. Then it hit me — ways I could come back home without finishing boot camp. I picked up my notebook and began to write down different scenarios.

First, I wrote I wanted to die, but I erased it because I realized how final it sounded. If I died, I couldn't enjoy my family anymore, ever. So, I gave a little more thought as to how to get out of the situation, knowing that death was too drastic. I proceeded to write, "I'll almost die." Next, I would win the Publisher's Clearing House Sweepstake, and with the winnings,

I would produce a television news show called Headline News. Lastly, I penned, "I'll act crazy," because I knew that was surely a way out. There was no way the Army was going to entrust me with a gun in that state of mind!

After writing all of that down, I ripped the page from the notebook and placed it in an envelope. I tucked the envelope inside the notebook and placed them in my mother's room for future reference. I had confidence it would be safe there. Soon after writing, sleep found me while I was still nervous about the day ahead.

Daylight broke through the darkness so soon; it was morning before I knew it. When I had awakened, I was not enthused at all. I had to leave my beloved boyfriend on Valentine's Day. (That's right, on February 14, 1995, I was leaving for boot camp!) My boyfriend and I had been dating for almost four years. We spent a lot of time together. Rarely was there a day we didn't spend with each other. He was indeed the guy I wanted to spend the rest of my life with. I loved his tall, slim physique. He had so much respect for me as a young woman. My boyfriend was a gentleman; he was a lot different from the previous guys I'd dated. Now, here I was leaving him behind!

Once I was dressed, my mother took me to the National Guard Armory in Hampton, South Carolina. We hugged and said our goodbyes after we arrived. I watched her drive away with a lump in my throat. I couldn't cry because I was a "soldier;" I was supposed to be tough! Shortly after my arrival at the Armory, we were called to get in formation. When everyone was accounted for, we went inside. The military personnel briefed me on small details. Then it was time to leave for Fort Jackson in Columbia, South Carolina. When we reached Orangeburg, South Carolina, I stalled the personnel from my unit by saying, "I need a toothbrush; I forgot mine." I knew it wouldn't change my orders to go, but I had to do something to delay my arrival.

They pulled into the parking lot of a Revco drugstore. I went inside and searched for the toothbrush aisle. Once I found it, I looked at every one of those toothbrushes and their prices just to further delay going to Fort Jackson. Finally, I picked one, headed to the checkout, and proceeded back to the car.

It seemed like the driver had put the pedal to the metal or time sped up because we arrived in Columbia very fast. When the Army personnel got me checked in, I got settled into the grim-looking hotel as best I could. My roommate went downstairs, and I stayed in the room for a while. The walls felt like they were closing in on me, so I went to the lobby to play card games with the other new recruits. It helped calm my nerves for a little while. After some time had passed, I returned to the room, and I stood in front of the mirror and said, "I wish I was pregnant." I knew the gentleman in my boyfriend wasn't going for that. There I was at nineteen years old, knowing for sure that I was in way too deep, and I should have listened to everyone who was trying to stop me from enlisting.

Morning dawned once more, with me more terrified now that the drill sergeants had arrived to take the other recruits and me on base. They instructed us to get on the bus, put our heads on the back of the seat in front of us, and keep our eyes closed.

One of the drill sergeants shouted, "Anyone caught with their eyes open will pay the consequence."

I sat in that seat with my eyes closed so tightly they began to hurt. All that yelling the drill sergeants were doing certainly put a lot of fear in me (it didn't take much to intimidate me) to convince me that they meant business! I was never a daredevil, and all chances of being one right then was not about to happen.

Well, my first few days were shaky. At this point, I no longer felt like myself, and it must have been obvious because I was sent to the psychologist for an evaluation. I found myself in the doctor's office, sitting on his chair and lying about not wanting to go back home. Convinced, he sent me back to the barracks to resume training. When we reached the gym, I remember overhearing some recruits saying if we failed the PT (physical training) exam, they would send soldiers home until we got fit enough to re-enlist. Aha! Since what I had written prior to coming to basic training wasn't coming to fruition quickly enough (so I thought), I decided to purposely fail the PT test.

The drill sergeant instructed everyone to get on the floor in position to do push-ups. *Oh yeah*, I thought, *I'm sure to fail this one*. My thoughts were rudely interrupted by the drill sergeant yelling in my face. "Down, Smalls.... Up!" How ironic, fear caused me to do perfect push-ups, sit-ups, etc. I passed the PT exam!

The next day, I remember being in a large room filled with at least one hundred recruits. The drill sergeant instructed us that he was going to call our numbers, and when we heard ours, he wanted us to stand. So, after the first few numbers being called, alas, I rose to my feet. Another recruit stood also. With his blustery voice, the drill sergeant turned to me and said, "What's your number, soldier?" I replied with my number. He said, "That's not the number I called. What are you, dyslexic, soldier? Go sit down!"

I thought *I guess I* am *dyslexic; I am terrified and everything else in between right now."* The embarrassment that came over me was so thick. At that point, my shot at having any confidence to finish basic training had jumped out of the window from the tallest building on base.

The drill instructor broke the recruits into different squads. When I entered the assigned small classroom setting, I felt bleak. A set of soldiers came in and asked if anyone felt like they couldn't proceed with training and needed to see a physician for any reason to be discharged. Suddenly, there was a ray of hope that sprung up in me. I thought here was another chance to get out of boot camp, so I politely raised my hand.

When I was given permission to speak, I told the soldiers that I was having excruciating pain from carrying the big duffle bag around. They sent me off to the physician. After my evaluation, and to my surprise, he gave me a prescription for pain pills and sent me back to the classroom to be assigned the work to do for that day. The job for that day turned out to be working with the dentist's office, sorting x-rays.

At the end of the workday, we returned to the barracks, and a female drill sergeant had us sit on the floor in front of her desk. I was sitting nearest the back. She said someone would get hot or cold. I didn't know who or what my drill sergeant was referencing because I couldn't concentrate. But as soon as the words left her mouth, my body demonstrated what was said. I suddenly became hot, then cold. I immediately knew something wasn't right, so I asked permission to go to the restroom. When I got there in the stall, I sat down on the toilet with my pants still up because I didn't have to urinate or anything. I just needed to try to figure out what was going on with me. Shortly after that, I passed out.

I heard another female private come to my aid, but she really didn't know what to do. The young lady ran out to get help for me. An older male dressed in camouflage with a wide rim hat was trying to wake me because I was in and out of consciousness. I was in the back of an ambulance fighting for my life when I came to. I heard the sirens blaring.

The EMT said to me, "Smalls, stay with us." He told the driver, "We've got to hurry."

Finally, we arrived at the Emergency Room. They tried to find a vein to draw blood. I was in and out again and totally oblivious to what was happening to me. The day came, and I *was* acting crazy; it was happening like I had journaled the night before boot camp!

Chapter 2

STOLE

I *WASN'T* "ACTING" crazy because what happened was real—no pretending. Something was very different about my character, and I realized it on the gurney as I was unable to utter a word. There was something strange going on inside of me. I felt exceptionally weak! *Everything* going on with me then was crazy.

In the emergency room, a white, short-haired, soft-spoken female lieutenant tried to keep me calm because, by this time, I was screaming, "I want to go home." What happened next, no one could have prepared me for. I had my eyes closed and started singing a familiar song I'd never heard myself sing so beautifully. My voice sounded angelic. Everyone back home would've agreed because I wasn't the best songstress in the church choir. Suddenly I sat up in the bed and yelled, "Hallelujah!" This voice that was coming from me didn't sound like me, but I certainly loved how melodious it sounded.

The lieutenant got me to lie back down. When I opened my eyes, I saw my buddy (the young lady assigned to me) crying. I asked my buddy, "Don't you want to go home with me?" Unknown to her, I wasn't speaking about my physical home in Yemassee, South Carolina, but a spiritual home in Heaven. As I closed my eyes again, a light brighter than any light I could describe appeared. It was easy on the eyes; it wasn't hurtful to look at directly like it was to look directly into the sun. Soon the light started to form into a silhouette. It became an image of a man, and a host of beings stood behind Him. He was now closer to me while the host of beings stayed afar off. I never saw detailed features of His face. The best way I could describe what I saw was when I saw a shadow of myself, but couldn't see my eyes, nose, skin color, etc., in the shadows. So it was with these lighted silhouettes standing before me when my eyes were closed.

I said, "Jesus, is that You? I want to go home with You!"

He softly answered, "No, you have to go back."

I pled more earnestly, "Jesus, please. I want to go with You."

Again, He said, "No, you have to go back. I have something for you to do."

I felt great in my spirit, but my physical mind was still running one hundred miles per hour. The soft-spoken lieutenant interrupted my conversation when she rubbed my left arm and said, "Everything is going to be all right." Things calmed down at this point, and the light silhouettes drifted away.

Apparently, they didn't just draw blood but gave me a shot to sedate me. I was so groggy; I could hardly keep my eyes open.

When I had gotten up to the floor where I would spend the next several days, a nurse and a soldier greeted me in a hallway, with a small table where I could check in my belongings. I took out $176.51 and realized the pain pills were gone. The nurse and soldier looked at each other and asked me to count what I had. After a couple of times counting, I couldn't remember how much I'd counted. I was on my third attempt to count when the nurse looked at the male soldier and told me to sign the document. I signed the sheet without reading over it. They escorted me to my room.

The next morning, I called my mom and told her what had happened and that I was in the hospital. She was upset. So, my mother and my boyfriend came to see me later that evening. I was so excited to be in their presence.

While I sat on my boyfriend's lap, and for no apparent reason, my nose began to bleed. My mother rushed out to get help, but as quickly as it had started, my nose stopped bleeding by the time the nurse came in. Their visit seemed short, but it could have very well been long. At this point, I really didn't know. Rational thinking was impaired, and I was heavily sedated.

I was sitting in the commons area three days after my mom and boyfriend's visit when I saw someone walk past the doorway with red, blue, and yellow balloons. The list I had made the night before I came to boot camp clicked in my mind, and this made me excited because I knew I had won the Publisher's Clearing House Sweepstake. After all, a few days before, two things on the list had come to pass. I almost died, and I was "acting crazy." I tried to figure out where the person went with my balloons. So, I thought maybe they wanted to surprise me when I returned to my room. In the meantime, I sat watching television and there it was: "Headline News" on cable TV. I couldn't believe it. I was rich from the sweepstakes winnings and had my very own television show! How could this be? I hadn't signed a check or talked to anyone about the plans I'd written prior to coming there.

Later, I attended group meetings, participated in activities, and conversed with other patients. After all that, I began to wonder where my prize was. A few days later, I finally started feeling like myself again. The doctors began processing the paperwork, preparing for my discharge, not just from the hospital but also from the military! Oh, I was elated when I found out that I didn't have to go back to basic training. I soon realized that the balloons weren't for me, and I didn't win the sweepstakes, and "Headline News" was on cable TV for quite some time (I didn't know that because my mom couldn't afford cable). My military discharge was more than winning the sweepstakes! It didn't matter because I was extremely ecstatic about going back to my hometown.

Wait, not so fast. I told those in charge of releasing me that they had spelled my first name wrong on my signed paperwork. They sent me downstairs to collect my belongings and said they would fix the error. The only thing I had was money, but to my surprise, the nurse and male soldier who collected my money the night I was committed stole $156.51 from me.

You are probably saying to yourself that I couldn't remember what I counted three times in their presence, so how could I possibly know exactly how much they stole? Or if they stole at all? Well, I had it written down in a notepad. I presented it to the attendant, but to no avail. The attendant insisted she could do nothing since I signed the document that night. I told the female lieutenant who coached me through in the E.R. that I could punch a brick wall. I walked out of that hospital with $20.

"Have you forgotten how we taught you to channel your emotions?" she asked.

I didn't respond because I was furious. I didn't want any discrepancies when it was time for me to officially leave. So, they sent me back to the barracks until my paperwork was corrected with the proper spelling of my first name. It dampened my spirit quite a bit, but I wanted everything done correctly.

Chapter 3

SQUARE ONE

ONCE I WAS discharged from the hospital and brought back to the barracks, I headed upstairs to the living quarters. I passed a couple of soldiers and a colonel and didn't salute. The colonel stopped and called out for me to turn around, so I did.

The colonel asked, "Why didn't you salute me?"

One of the soldiers with her said, "Oh, that's Smalls. She just got out of the hospital."

The three of them chuckled, and the colonel said, "Oh, well, carry on."

I realized that my unfortunate circumstance was amusement for them, making me feel worthless and more embarrassed. I reverted to my discharge, which brought me back to a happy place.

Meanwhile, fixing the error with my name was taking longer than I expected. I had to pack my things and be relocated to another set of barracks, where I remained on base for at least two more days. Thankfully, I was no longer at the initial barracks where I was the brunt of everyone's jokes. However, I settled into the other barrack that looked like a dungeon. It was indeed creepy in every sense of the word. Later, I was called downstairs to meet a visitor. I wondered who it could possibly be. When I got down there, I recognized him immediately. It was a sergeant from back home. He told me that my mom had called his sister and explained what happened to me; my mom wanted him to check on me since she hadn't heard from me since her visit. He advised me to call my mom and tell her I would be coming home the next day.

I headed back up the creepy stairway to use the payphone. My mom was excited to hear from me and even more happy that I was coming home the next day, late that evening. My mother said she would try to plan to pick me up from the bus station in Yemassee because she had to work when I was scheduled to arrive. So, my mom suggested she might come to get me that morning because it was only a two-hour drive from Yemassee to Fort Jackson. It would take four to six hours to get back home by bus. My mother's suggestion meant she would have been to work that evening, and I would have arrived home hours earlier. I declined her offer simply so she wouldn't have to spend money she really didn't have.

After our brief conversation, it was time for the other discharged soldiers and me to go on yard duty. We raked and picked up pinecones all day. When we finished, we went to the mess hall to eat and from there to the gym to play basketball and use the exercise equipment.

Square One

Although I was exhausted from the hard work in the yard and playing basketball, I hardly slept that night because of the anticipation of going home. It kept me up, thinking about what my next move would be since the funds for college were still unattainable. I got up that next morning and did all the usual hygiene stuff. When I was ready, I went downstairs, never looking back. I only had the taxicab in view. I arrived at the bus station and told the attendant I would be with him all day until my bus came.

He looked at my ticket and said, "I see you are going to Yemassee. I live not far from there in Grays. Let me see if I can get you on another bus close to Yemassee." I wanted to jump for joy, but I kept my composure while holding my breath in hopes that there was an earlier time available. I was so ready to leave Columbia, South Carolina.

The nice young man looked up from his computer screen and said, "I have a bus coming in an hour-and-a-half, going to Hampton." Hampton was only sixteen miles from Yemassee. "There will be an hour layover in Orangeburg. Would you like for me to change your ticket?"

I answered with a resounding "Yes!" before he could finish the question. Of course, I immediately got on the phone and told my mom there was a change of plans. The four-hour trek back home would be long and boring, but I didn't care, because I was now getting home hours earlier than first scheduled. This darling young lady would get home mid-afternoon instead of late that night.

Only like my mother would do initially, she automatically thought something bad had happened. I quickly told her no; I was coming home earlier than scheduled. Now I had to go through all the details. My mom rearranged her time at work so that she could be in Hampton to get me personally.

I told her, "When I get there, I will kiss the ground." My mother didn't think all that was necessary, but she didn't *know* all that I had been through those few weeks; it was going to be worth it to me.

In the meantime, I went down the street to get some Chinese food with a couple of young ladies who came with me from the base. It didn't take me long to eat, nor did I hang around for conversation, with chances of missing my bus. I talked while I was eating. When I finished, I walked alone back to the bus station. Shortly after returning, my bus pulled up. I got butterflies in my stomach from the excitement. When it was time to board the bus, I was first in line.

When the bus arrived in Orangeburg, there was a short layover, as the attendant in Columbia had said. People wanted to browse around the city and asked if I would watch their stuff. I agreed without hesitation because I was not going to leave the spot I was sitting in, not even to use the restroom. There was no way I was going to miss the next bus. The hour went by so fast. Yippy! As we headed down the highway, I thanked God for getting me out of the mess I had put myself into. My body was tired, and my eyes were heavy, so I closed them to take a nap. I woke up, realizing I was almost in Hampton. I felt like a kid on Christmas morning with anticipation of seeing all the gifts under the tree.

Hampton was on the horizon. We were getting closer and closer. The sights were getting more and more familiar. Finally, the bus pulled into the station. There was my mom, one of my aunts, and my two little sisters. As I was going to retrieve my bags, I knelt in that oily parking lot and kissed the ground. I hugged my family. My mom, of course, couldn't believe I kissed the ground.

"Don't you know germs are on that pavement? You could get sick," she fussed.

I smiled and thought, *Well, if I do, the doctors have antibiotics*. I simply said, "Let's go home!"

The family wanted details of what happened as we drove home to Yemassee. I shared as much as I could, then, and in the days ahead.

Within the time allotted, I went to the Armory to return the things issued to me at basic training. That was such a burden off my shoulders. The events that had occurred were still heavily haunting me in my mind. I was embarrassed, felt worthless, and doubted my capability of doing anything right, more times than I cared to remember. I slipped into a silent depression. I was smiling on the outside but deeply wounded inside, crying only when God was watching. I was back to square one—jobless.

Chapter 4

RAMS IN THE BUSH

BECAUSE I WAS so depressed, I didn't go out looking for a job, even though I knew I desperately needed one. Similar to Abraham, who knew he needed a different sacrifice other than his son, God provided a ram in the bush (Gen. 22). I needed a different kind of job besides the military. So, one sweet day, one of my cousins, my ram in the bush, came to me unexpectedly before I killed my self-confidence. He asked if I would like to work at the Shell Gas Station where he was employed. I said yes, but I wasn't totally convinced I could be good at it. I applied anyway, and I got the job. So, a little less than a month after returning from boot camp, I was employed, just like that.

One night after work, I went to visit my boyfriend. We were watching a movie, and it was good until it got near the end. I began sobbing and walked outside. He knew I was emotional, but this was different because I'd never walked out before. He followed me outside and asked what had happened. I told him the way the character was gasping for air as he was dying reminded me of what happened on my way to the E.R. that day at boot camp. He embraced me with reassurance that everything would be okay, but only he knew I was breathing, yet I felt like I was dying inside.

Daily the thoughts of almost dying were asphyxiating my known ability to succeed. I was keeping busy with work and going on dates with my boyfriend, but I didn't feel complete. I was empty and needed some fulfillment. It seemed like going to church wasn't helping me either, so I stopped going cold turkey. I decided I would go back to college, even though I still couldn't afford it, even with financial aid. I needed new scenery and a fresh start. The decision was final, so I gave my boss two weeks' notice after working there for only three months.

I was courteous enough to work on the holiday of July 4th. Within the next few days, my boyfriend and I moved to Statesboro, Georgia, in hopes of becoming students of Georgia Southern University again. He found a job easily, while I on the other hand was living torpidly around the apartment. Day after day went by, and I couldn't get motivated to look for a job. A friend of my boyfriend's (another ram in the bush) asked if I wanted a job at Burger King. Well, I'd been in Statesboro for two months jobless, and this was my chance to help out with the bills, so I accepted his offer. How hard could it be to work at Burger King?

I began working on a Thursday morning during the breakfast and partial lunch hours. I was overwhelmed with the people's orders. Too many of them wanted to have it their way. I shouted in my head, *Take it the way it comes, and if you don't like something, don't eat it; take it off the sandwich.* I told the manager around day four that I had a family emergency with my mom and needed to go back home. I didn't give her a two weeks' notice. I told her I would be quitting in the next three days. After all, it was an "emergency."

That same day, while I was on break, one of the employees, a tall, dark elderly man, the janitor, asked if I was in Statesboro going to school. I said not at the present time because I didn't have enough money to cover tuition after financial aid. He asked another question that set off all alarms and whistles that I really needed to go back home to my mom. He asked in a tender, grandfatherly voice, "Who are you living with?"

I answered, "I'm living with a friend." He poured gas on the fire he'd started by asking, "A friend or a *boyfriend*?" I knew what he was getting at because I was questioning my morals too. I was living in sin.

I stood there ashamed again, but for a different reason. My morals were now at stake. From time to time, my mother and pastor taught the lesson not to "shack" before marriage. Still, I had thrown that principle out the window as I rode down the highway to Statesboro with my boyfriend. I went home that afternoon and cried, with guilt deep in my heart. The one-bedroom apartment was so small, and there was no place to retreat to for privacy at moments like this, so I went into the closet.

My boyfriend found me in there in tears when he came from work. My eyes were puffy and hurting from all the crying. I explained to him the conversation I had with the co-worker.

He agreed that he was starting to feel guilty about shacking too. I confessed that I would be quitting my job in three days and wanted to return home to Yemassee the next weekend. Eventually, he tried to talk me out of the closet, but to no avail. He walked out and went into the living room. When I was sure he wasn't coming right back in, I came out of the closet and sat on the side of the bed. I listened to "Be Encouraged" by William Becton. The more I listened, the less encouraged I became. Guilt had now taken a grip on me also!

It was final: Burger King's slogan was taken way too seriously for me, and living in sin was no longer an option. I worked that Wednesday morning, got my check, and headed back to the apartment to start packing my things. On Friday, my boyfriend took me back to South Carolina. Neither one of us had any regrets about the decision I had made. I promised to help him with the rent once I started working again.

I went back to the Shell gas station to work in just two weeks. I stayed there for five months. So, once again, I was back to the drawing board, trying to figure out where my life was heading. I sat around the house feeling sorry for myself when my godfather (the third ram in the bush) paid me a visit. He asked if I wanted to work at his and his wife's bridal store. I was a little hesitant because I knew that would require me to dress up. Everybody knew I was a jeans and T-shirt kind of girl. I told him I would give it a try.

I quit the Shell gas station again and decided to work for my godparents. I worked in the bridal store for two days and asked if it was possible that I could work in the beauty supply store they had next door. It wasn't because I had to dress up, although I lied and said it was, but the young lady who was supposed to be training me wasn't teaching me anything. Perhaps she felt threatened because the owners were my godparents, but I would not have caused her any trouble if only she had gotten to know me. So, a few days later, I was hired at the beauty supply store, getting trained by my god-brother and another employee.

I liked the job so much and did it so well that they gave me the keys to open since I was always waiting for them to open the door. My confidence was building for the first time in a long time. I was trusted to be responsible for a store with thousands of dollars worth of merchandise. At this point, I wasn't a Christian, but I was brought up with Christian values, even though I didn't come from a Christian home. I went to church, but Christ wasn't in me. I reverenced God and believed He was sovereign, but there was no commitment to Him from me. My mom and the Sunday School teacher taught me to be honest. So, my godparents saw that quality in me and trusted me with the keys to their store.

This job didn't open on Sundays. This allowed my family and me to start attending church again regularly. Church was no longer church as usual since boot camp. I was listening to what the pastor had to say. I was in the choir, lending my voice because I really didn't know how to stay in my key. So, I lent it to the sopranos, the altos, and the tenors in different parts of the song because that was where I felt comfortable at those moments (when the choir director really wanted me to stay in soprano). Monday mornings, when I had to work, I was refueled from Sunday's sermon and looked forward to the next.

Chapter 5

THE PIVOTAL POINT

As TIME MOVED along, one fateful evening in March 1996, my boyfriend proposed after we'd been dating for almost five years. I was happy as a lark because I had given him an ultimatum late in the prior year and wasn't sure what his choice was going to be. I knew I didn't want to become another statistic, joining the young women who lost their purity and the men in their lives walked away. I was more in love with him than with what God had said about fornication. The risk of giving my boyfriend an ultimatum apparently had turned in my favor. I would soon be his wife! This relieved me so much.

Although I had said we wouldn't be engaged sexually when I moved back to South Carolina from Statesboro, Georgia, I was still weak and needed some help. Church seemed like it would take too much effort, too many rules to follow, and too much of my time away from my boyfriend. Well, for months, my boyfriend-now-turned-fiancé and I "knew" each other a lot and enjoyed every moment of it. God was the only One I knew who could take the desire away, but I wasn't ready to surrender my life to Jesus Christ.

The wedding date had been set for December 20, 1998. Since the proposal, my mom, sisters, and I would shop endlessly for my wedding. My sisters would sometimes be frustrated with the length of time we would stay in the stores. My mom and I had to coax them many times by assuring them that they would be rewarded if they didn't rush us. Since they were teenagers, you would have thought they would love shopping, but I guess they would have rather been with their boyfriends some of those Saturdays.

Thankfully, I was still working with my godparents, who owned the bridal store, because they deeply discounted my beaded wedding gown. That was such a blessing. On Sunday, April 28, 1996, became a pivotal point in my life, as detail after detail was being finalized over the next two years and eight months.

I was at church, being attentive to some of the things being said. In late March, I was still so full of the Seven Last Words program when each preacher spoke on the seven things Jesus Christ said on the cross. At that program, speaker after speaker was talking directly to me about how Christ had died for my sins. As I reflected on the church program in March that Sunday morning in April, I was in a zone in the choir. When the invitation to Christ was extended, one of the choir members looked to me and whispered, "You know you want to do it, so go ahead. I can see it all over you." I made the conscious choice to go down to the small brown-stained altar to give my life to Christ, as my Lord and my Savior.

The pastor asked me why I wanted to give my life to Christ. I remember saying some people might think I was too young to be standing here, but... (I paused, choking back tears) I went on to tell my story of how God had come to me while I was in the hospital at boot camp. As I was speaking, a light had encompassed me, and it felt like it was God and me in the church alone. After the testimony, I went into a time of praise, much like the one I'd had in the hospital, only this time I shouted "Hallelujah!" a lot more.

I felt tears coming down my face, and then a lady grabbed me from behind and whispered in my ear that that was enough. I said, "I rebuke you, Satan, in the name of Jesus." She turned me loose.

Another lady had said to her, "She's okay. Let her praise God." I saw one guy leave because he had had enough. This was the first time in perhaps a long time, if not ever, this had happened in our tiny, red-brick United Methodist church. That very day, He (Jesus) took the desire from me to cuss and have sex before marriage. Weeks later, unknown to me, I found out that during my testimony, I was speaking in tongues. I thought the congregation heard my account of what happened at boot camp because that was exactly what I was saying when the light surrounded me. Maybe that was why the lady attempted to quiet me when I spoke in tongues, and the man left.

On Monday, my fiancé came to pick me up to drop him off at work in Walterboro, and then I would proceed an hour back to Beaufort to my job. I told him about my commitment to Christ the day before and my vow not to have sex with him until we were married. It shouldn't have been a surprise that he agreed, because after all, he concurred with my decision to come back home from Statesboro when he didn't feel comfortable with our living arrangements anymore either.

I was feeling refreshed. I told the pastor a few Sundays later that I'd had an urge to go to Bible college to study the Bible so I'd be able to teach God's word. He was moved by that, and the week following, he got me a teacher's Sunday school guide to implement in class. So, there I was, teaching Sunday school in such a short period of time without any formal training, teaching the adults and children regularly. Indeed, I was enjoying what I was doing.

In the meantime, between studying lessons and getting things finalized for the wedding (with a month to go), I was side-tracked. I was waiting for a family vacation meeting at my aunt's (my mom's sister) house when my mother called us from her sickbed with sad news. On that cool fall evening, my ninety-four-year-old great-grandaunt passed away.

I was so sad because I had just seen her earlier that day. I was definitely concerned by the way she had looked. Her body was back to the size I knew it to be when I was a child. Still, I didn't think she was dying, and the nurses didn't tell me or the others when I inquired about her hands being so pale and swollen. I was too young and naïve to understand the technical terms of her condition. My great-grandaunt's hands were blown up like clear balloons, so the ring on her ring finger was impossible to remove. I thought her face would pop from the swelling. I couldn't get the image out of my mind. She was our prayer warrior even while she was in the nursing home. We didn't know how significant a role she played in our lives until she passed away, and things went terribly wrong at church shortly after that.

Chapter 6

UNEXPECTED REVIVAL VISITORS

THE FUNERAL ARRANGEMENTS had been made, and it had come time for my mom to retrieve our aunt's belongings from the nursing home in Walterboro. As we walked into the lobby on a Tuesday afternoon, my baby sister said, "There's our aunt right there."

I turned to her and asked, "What did you say?"

"Oh nothing," she quickly replied. My other sister and I looked at each other. We repeated what our baby sister had said, only to confirm that neither of us imagined what we had heard.

Once we'd gotten everything and returned to Yemassee from the nursing home in Walterboro, my brother, my second youngest sister, and I decided to go to the revival at our church. Some people didn't think it was such a great idea since we were grieving, but nothing could keep me from church that night. Everything at church on that cool November night had seemed normal, up until the point when the guest female pastor got up and began to speak.

She said, "I don't have any notes tonight to read from." She started talking about a doomsday clock in London, England, that was about to strike twelve, and the world would be no more. My brother and I became very unsettled in our spirits at this point.

I couldn't believe this woman was up there predicting the end of the world by a clock. After she'd been speaking on the subject for a few minutes, she pulled out her notes, which she'd said she didn't have and began to read from them. The parishioners in there were in a trance, including our pastor. Only a few had looked like they weren't into what she was saying. At this time, I heard an evil voice bounce off the wall and pierce my inner ear.

"She knows we are in here. Let's go to the back," the voice said.

I turned to my brother and said, "I can't breathe. Something hit off the wall into my right ear."

He could see that my lips were white, and my face was pale, so he simply said, "Breathe."

I stood up and said to the female speaker, "I rebuke you in the name of Jesus." My brother got up from his seat, and on his way to the altar, he said he saw a huge demon. It was muscular from its neck down to its legs. He described being drawn to the altar by a force, which he acknowledges now as the Holy Spirit, to pray. Once he was at the altar, there was pressure on both his shoulders that led him to kneel at the altar. He was there alone, praying; no one else joined him.

In the meantime, I tried to get our pastor's attention at the pulpit to tell him this lady needed to be stopped, but the more I called for him, the more he was zoned into what she was saying. The atmosphere was so gloomy. The heaviness of darkness was making the lighting dimmer and dimmer.

Finally, our pastor came and sat next to me, but his eyes were still fixed on this woman. I punched him in his right arm, but he ignored me. I asked an usher for some water. When I was drinking it, I began to choke. So, I proceeded to spit it out. I looked around the room and saw that a lady from our sister church was observing me. I asked her to sing the song "Holy Spirit, You're Welcome in this Place." She began the song reluctantly, and the congregation started helping but they really didn't know what was going on in there. There were unexpected revival visitors—demons—warring with the Spirit.

When church was dismissed, I was standing on the front steps, and an older cousin came to me and said the female speaker wanted me to come to the pastor's study so she and I could talk.

I emphatically responded with, "No. I am not going back there with her!" Shortly after that, I saw her leave in her car, without another word to me or the pastor. My pastor sensed something did indeed happen to me and told my brother and sister that he would drive me back to our mom's house.

I don't remember our conversation that night. All I knew was at that moment, something was different about me. I felt like I did at boot camp, but it was more intense. When the pastor and I got to the house, my mom noticed it too and later told me she had thought, *Not again*. She wasn't feeling well but recognized that I was not talking and behaving like myself. I was saying there was a new prophet in town (referring to my mom) and sat next to her like a small child in need of her mommy's attention. She decided I needed to go to the hospital to be evaluated.

Chapter 7

THE POWER OF PRAYER

WHILE I WAS sitting in the backseat of the car between a couple of relatives, waiting to go to the hospital, I looked out the window and saw someone standing there with a cream, crocheted sweater on.

The devil said, "That's your great-grandaunt."

I could see she was about to lean over to look in, but I became afraid and said, "No, no, that's not my aunt." I wanted to hide my face, but I couldn't because it felt like there were vice grips on my arms. As soon as I was about to turn my head away, the person I thought was the devil leaned completely down to the window, and I sighed in relief that it was only an older female cousin. After having a few words with her, my mom got into the car so that we could leave to go to Beaufort Memorial Hospital.

Oh, my Lord, this had seemed like the darkest night ever! We drove down the ten-mile stretch of road with many mossy oak trees hanging over. When we came to a stop and turned onto Highway 17 to bear onto Highway 21, we approached Whale Branch Bridge another five miles down the road. I feared we were going to go over the side of the bridge. Everyone in the car did their best to keep me calm. When we got to the traffic light by Chinatown Chinese Restaurant in Beaufort, South Carolina, I felt like we were going up steep hills and coming down into deep valleys, although the road was flat. I could see red lightning flashing in the dark night sky.

This went on slowly as we approached the hospital five more miles down the road. I wanted to sit in the car long enough to listen to the rest of Dottie People's song, "Handwriting on the Wall." When it was over, they took me inside the Emergency Room. I asked to go to the restroom, and once inside, I couldn't believe my eyes. I saw scratches on my arm and my lips looked bruised like I had been biting them. Upon returning to the lobby, the nurse called me to the back.

I sat in a chair in this small room with a few of my loved ones around me. Every time my uncle's wife touched the back of my neck, I felt like something disgusting was crawling on me, and I felt like I was on fire. With my eyes closed, I saw blood all around. I got agitated. It felt like I was being dipped into cool water when my mom touched me. That happened a few times while the nurse was in the room, and it continued while she was gone. I was very agitated and had no self-control. I was having a "nervous breakdown." The nurse came back with the needle to give me a shot; I hit the floor so hard everyone gasped, and my mom said, "Oh my God! Did she break any bones?"

Thankfully, I had not. I was in the hospital for a while for observation to see how I would react to the shot. I was groggy from it and had no signs of an allergic reaction, so I was discharged. My family and I went outside and formed a circle to pray, but there was somebody there I had never seen before. I was instructed to hold his hand, and when I did, I felt uneasy.

I told my mom, "I can't hold his hand. Something's not right. His eyes are like blood."

She was frustrated and said, "Hold his hand, or do you want to go back into the hospital? He's your uncle and aunt's pastor. Your aunt called him to come to pray for you."

Against my will, I held his hand and felt uneasy while he prayed.

After being discharged and praying in the hospital's parking lot, I returned to my mom's house, still feeling a little agitated. I didn't want to be left alone to bathe or fall asleep because I was so fearful. My mom accompanied me in the bathroom as I washed, and she laid down next to me in her bed. I dozed off finally, but I was awakened to a feeling like something was crawling on me. My mom later explained that she had seen knots form in my arm, which moved back and forth. She had opened the Bible, placed it under my head, and began to pray. The next morning, my behavior and speech weren't any better than the night before, even though I was less agitated.

She took me back to the hospital late the following Wednesday night. This time they admitted me into the mental health ward in the wee hours of Thursday morning, but not without opposition from the doctors. Apparently, the hospital staff wanted to send me to a state mental hospital in Columbia, but my mom was adamant about me staying in Beaufort. In fact, the hospital records said I was transferred to Bryan Psychiatric Hospital for further care, but I was *never* there. The county sheriff was called, and he defused the situation after hearing my mother's reason for pushing so hard for me to stay there in Beaufort, rather than two hours away—she was preparing our aunt's funeral. The sheriff's compassion toward my mother got her what she'd been pleading for with Beaufort Memorial Hospital's staff—to keep me in Beaufort.

I repeatedly told the nurses and the doctor that I couldn't stay there because I had a funeral to go to that Friday, and my wedding was December 20, 1998, at 5:00 PM. (I was unaware at the time, but my fiancé told me several months later that family had asked him if he was sure he still wanted to marry me.) Although I was heavily medicated and drowsy, I remained adamant with the staff about not staying in there for the three days they stated. While I was confident about not being there past Thursday night, a very powerful prayer was sent up on my behalf at my mother's house in the meantime.

I was told that a deacon from the Missionary Baptist Church in Yemassee and a few other visitors came by Mom's house to find her upset because the doctor had just told her that he would keep me in the hospital for another two to three days. The deacon offered to pray, and my mother accepted. My brother left the living room and entered our mother's room to pray alone. He said he couldn't hear the deacon's words, but it sounded like thunder. At some point, my brother ended his own prayer and began to have a vision. When he looked up, an angel was hovering in the eastern corner of the room with a sword drawn warring with a beast/demon.

The angel said in a thunderous voice to my brother, "It is finished. Go get your sister."

The deacon's prayer had ended also. The angel looked at my brother and smiled after he stabbed the beast/demon. My brother saw the angel return the sword into its sheath while the beast/demon remained lying at the angel's feet. The vision faded away.

My brother returned to the living room with the others and said to our mom, "You can now go get Lexsis because it is finished."

My mom said, "I'm going to get Lexsis."

My uncle and a distant cousin accompanied my mother to the hospital to make sure she didn't lose her cool with the staff. Still, to their surprise, my uncle and cousin weren't allowed to go with her to speak to the doctor. I was sitting at the table facing the door and having lunch in the kitchen. I saw my mom walk to the nurse's station. I first thought I should run out to meet her because I was so excited to see her.

Then, the Holy Spirit spoke to me softly, "No, don't run out there because they will think you are crazy. Stay here."

I was obedient to the Spirit of the living God. I sat there and finished my lunch. Soon after, the head counselor and my mom came into the kitchen to talk with me. Shortly after that, the counselor left and returned with the discharge papers. On that Thursday afternoon, I was discharged against medical advice.

The hospital staff simply couldn't override the power of prayer that was sent up on my behalf a few hours earlier.

Chapter 8

THE FUNERAL

ONCE I HAD gotten home from the hospital, my mom was trying to decide if I should go to the funeral or not.

The same cousin who went with her to the hospital told my mom, "Let's take her to the funeral home to see her great-grand-aunt and observe her reaction."

I was still groggy from the medication, so I don't remember crying like my mom said I did, but I do recall smiling and saying, "She's so pretty." I didn't attend the wake service that Thursday evening because I was resting for the funeral the next day.

While my mom was out handling personal business, she left another one of my uncles in charge of me. Knowing my condition, my uncle tried to use it to his advantage by asking me to do things, like cut him a piece of cake that wasn't supposed to be cut at the time because it was for the funeral's repast. He thought he had me cornered, but I wasn't that out of it to cut that cake!

The YOUNG *and the* RESTED

Friday, November 20, 1998, was a beautiful fall day. The sky was mostly clear, and the air was so refreshingly crisp. I awoke from a good night's sleep, only to argue with my mom about going to the funeral. She insisted that I should stay home with my uncle and was determined that I wasn't going to. As she and I went back and forth about me staying or going, I was getting my clothes ready. I showered and came back into the room to get dressed.

My mother was getting upset, so she went and got my uncle (who had gone to the hospital with her) to talk to me. But before he could come, I was completely dressed and walking down the tiny hall. My brother was kneeling on the floor, pleading with our mom.

He said, "She gotta go, Rie."

Our mom told my uncle, "Now I have two of them on my hands," thinking that my brother had lost it too.

I turned to her and said, "I'll help you with him."

Looking back at that moment now is so hilarious because how was I going to help with my brother if I was still a little groggy from the medicine?

The family was gathering outside the house for the funeral line-up. I was content as can be while my mom was indoors, upset over my decision to go to the funeral. She gave up arguing with me, not wanting to cause a scene since the funeral director and family members were already at the house. I proceeded to the funeral with my family. Once we got there, it was an experience like no other. Even the pastor was in awe because he said he'd never hit a casket while doing the eulogy in all his pastoral years.

The first thing that amazed me about my great-grandaunt's funeral was that the sanctuary doors were never closed, and it wasn't because people were standing outside; the ushers just never shut them. The brilliant sun rays shone through the doors and windows, reminding me of the day I gave my life to Christ and was engulfed in light, speaking to God. The second thing was that after the pastor stated his text "The Truth," which was taken from John 8:32-44, he hammered it home that the truth shall set you free while hitting his fist on the casket three times. The pastor was surprised that he'd done that. Once the funeral was over, he said he had never done that before. It was clear that he really wanted all of us to know that Jesus is the truth and He will set us free if we trust and believe. Truly, that day even unbelievers were touched by the service.

Lastly, after the sermon and shouts of praise unto God, it came time to view the body. I sat quietly watching the people in a single-file line go by the casket, one by one. Most seemed to be happy rather than sorrowful, maybe because they knew my aunt was a godly woman and that she had gone on to be with the Lord. My brother and I were responsible for closing the casket for the final time. He and I had tucked everything back in the casket when I, for some odd reason, decided to lean in and kiss our aunt on the cheek and said, "Bye, Bo." That was something we often said when we departed each other's presence. When I realized I'd just kissed a dead body, a part of me snapped back to complete sanity.

I had never done that (kiss a dead body) before or ever again. It seemed a bit creepy to me. After the burial, though I was completely back to thinking clearly, there was something different about how my body felt. I observed my immediate family, and they looked like how I was feeling.

I thought, *Could this really be?*

The next day, we took my nieces to a fall carnival at the elementary school and I was still feeling weird.

Finally, I asked one of my sisters, "Do you feel like we are moving in slow motion, like zombies?"

"Yes, I thought it was just me," she said.

After the carnival, we went back by my grandmother's house. A family friend from Greenville, South Carolina, appeared out of nowhere. He came with bags of fruit and candy, and the lattice I'd requested for my wedding. Later that day, he took my sisters and a friend of theirs around the community to distribute the fruit bags to the elderly and other children. As a few days passed, what we all knew as normalcy came back because the final touches on my wedding were needed.

There were a few hiccups in finalizing the wedding details, but I was determined not to let Satan reign. A month after the funeral, on Sunday, December 20, 1998, I married my best friend, with a slightly heavy heart that my great-grandaunt couldn't be there. Despite that fact, the wedding ceremony left people touched by the love in the air that my husband and I shared.

Chapter 9

NOT MY SISTER TOO

FOUR YEARS HAVE passed since my wedding. Everything had been wonderful. My husband and I had had our first son and were expecting our youngest son. Then all hell broke loose at a women's conference in Tampa, Florida. Surely, I didn't expect the things that happened to occur. I watched my sister have a mental meltdown at one of the sessions. I heard a conversation between Satan and God as my sister spoke.

Satan angrily said through her, "She is mine."

God, calmly but with authority, said, "No, she isn't."

"I hate You, God," Satan said in frustration.

She later explained that when I heard the conversation and a young man had come over to help her, she could see how he was abusive to women. Eventually, she was transported to a hospital.

When my mother and I arrived in her hospital room, I could immediately tell Satan had taken over because my sister's demeanor was nothing like usual.

My sister's eyes were different when she looked at me and said, "Did you miss me?"

I knew it wasn't her speaking because she sounded so wicked. I said no to Satan and left the room. My mom stayed in the room with my sister while I was in the hall, talking to one of the doctors. I was trying to tell him that she wasn't on illegal drugs and that this was indeed spiritual warfare.

My mom was informed later in the evening that my sister would have to stay in the hospital's mental ward for at least three days. I was devastated. I couldn't believe this was happening to my sister too. I began to have that feeling again like I did in 1996 and 1998. I didn't say anything to anybody because I was afraid. I simply confessed to two other ladies who came with us to the conference that I had two previous nervous breakdowns and knew what my sister was going through.

The following day while we were in the last conference session, my mom got a phone call saying my sister was going to be discharged. In the meantime, I was secretly having my own meltdown. After the session, we headed to the van, and I saw my sister and became afraid of her because of what happened at the hospital. I didn't know if she was well enough to make the trip back home. Now I was frightening my son during the ride back to South Carolina because I wasn't behaving like the mom he knew.

When we stopped to eat on our way from Tampa, things got more and more bizarre with me. Once we exited the restaurant and returned to the vehicle, I lay down in the front seat of the van, looking up in the sky and seeing an image of a baby in the womb.

God said to me, "The baby you are carrying is fine."

I was so thankful to hear Him say that! A day or two after reaching South Carolina, my family told me I ran away from my mom's house to the busy highway. I couldn't be caught by my youngest sister. I eventually ran back to the house. Then I climbed the wall in my mother's master bathroom. Once I was settled in the living room, seated in a chair, I was hallucinating; I saw my husband dressed in the tuxedo he had worn to his senior prom. He was called while all this was happening. When he reached my mother's house, he decided not to go another day without getting me some help. He called 911 because I was completely broken down mentally. When the ambulance arrived, my husband rode in the back with me as I was taken to the hospital in Hampton, South Carolina.

After a lengthy discussion with me, the staff decided that I should go to Columbia's mental institution, but they found out I was two months pregnant. They then decided to send me to Beaufort Memorial Hospital over in the next county.

I was handcuffed and put into the back of a police patrol car since I was so agitated and wouldn't quietly sit still in the Emergency Room. The officers transported me to Yemassee, South Carolina, where an old, frustrated officer met them. The old officer re-handcuffed me so tightly that it left black and blue bruises on my wrists. When he got me to the hospital, he dragged me to the front entrance and told me to sit in the first chair. I was so afraid. I was shortly admitted and wheeled to the mental ward. In the double-door room they placed me in, I repeatedly said, "God is in control, and He will never leave me or forsake me."

Things seemed unreal to me when I was discharged, even though what I remembered was so vivid. I questioned myself for days on whether or not that police officer dragged me to the hospital's entrance that night, so I finally asked my mom if it were true.

She said, "Yes, the next day, he was bragging to your uncle about how he had dragged a crazy lady into the hospital the night before. Of course, your uncle had some *choice* words for him when he told the officer that the 'crazy' lady was you—his niece."

They all thought I should have sued him, but I decided to let God handle him. I saw the officer at a relative's funeral shortly after this ordeal. He didn't even recognize me, nor did I try to make myself known.

Chapter 10

You are Bipolar

When I returned home to Georgia, I had to do a follow-up visit with my physician. Well, this would be the first time I would meet this man. After he read my medical records, I finally heard these words:

"You are bipolar. These weren't just nervous breakdowns you were having. You need medication to balance you."

I was stunned because that was not what I wanted to hear, and I was certainly not ready to believe it. All I could think about was how people would treat me once they learned of my bipolar diagnosis.

I had heard the snide remarks people had made about bipolar individuals, and I didn't want to live under that stigma. So, I refused to believe I was bipolar and brushed it off as a few nervous breakdowns. I even refused to take the medicine I had been prescribed because it was like admitting that I had a mental problem. At that time, I was embarrassed to come to grips with such a condition. I didn't want family and friends to treat me differently or scorn me. I'd seen others with bipolar disorder mistreated, and I didn't want to take medicine that would make me noticeably lethargic.

I went on and had a healthy baby boy in March of the following year. I was feeling fine mentally and physically without taking any medicines. I convinced myself that I was healed miraculously.

Then 2004 rolled around, and I had another episode. I began to question my "miraculous healing." I believed I'd done everything right to please God, but here I was, having another episode! To my amazement, I was admitted into the hospital, released the same day, and given an antipsychotic prescription to take for a few days. I wanted this to be the last hospital visit because I didn't like being there or the episodes I experienced. I was determined not to go back!

In May 2005, while I thumbed through the pages of my journal, I was on the onset of having another breakdown. I could tell by my handwriting that I was manic at times because it was sometimes barely legible, and I *wrote* in more than one journal. I was having breakthroughs (periods of being rational) leading up to the next episode. At the end of May 2005, during one of these breakthroughs, I was reading in one journal and found where God had given me this book title. I wrote down, *The Young and the Rested* because, at that point, I was tired of these episodes, and I wanted rest. I was very serious about writing. I even started writing a little about my childhood, back when my great-grandmother was still alive, but I couldn't get a rhythm going. My writing was aimless and very difficult, so I stopped abruptly. I admitted that I had no clue what I was doing, and sadly, I didn't ask anyone for help, mainly because I didn't know who to ask.

I narrowly escaped being admitted to the mental health unit in May 2005, when I visited my brother there. God knew our mother couldn't handle that, so He spared me. Yes, you heard me right. My pea in the pod had a bipolar episode too. At this time, I was sporadically taking my medicine, and by November, I had just stopped taking it altogether.

Chapter 11

DENIAL

I HAD NOT come to grips with my diagnosis, although all the signs and behaviors were there. Denial was at its best in me at that time. Before, it was simply that I didn't know why or what was going on, but now I was embarrassed. I didn't want to be labeled as mentally ill, which is often translated by others as "crazy."

In April 2006, I had a vision of seeing myself on a television screen, where Alan Alda from the TV series *M*A*S*H* was watching me go through a bipolar episode. I was running around confused and in a psychotic state. I collapsed onto the floor, lay there in a fetal position, and cried. Mr. Alda was in tears as he watched helplessly. I was unsure why I had a vision with Mr. Alda in it, but I speculated that God wanted me to see myself as others saw me while I went through the breakdowns.

In the meantime, off and on, I had been going to a godly counselor but wouldn't do as he, my physician, and my husband had all told me to do and take my medicine. So inevitably, on Monday, December 18, 2006, I was admitted once again into the hospital's mental unit. I was stunned. It was two days before my eighth wedding anniversary.

On December 20, 2006, I realized that I really wasn't going to spend my anniversary with my husband. This time, I didn't get out on the same day I was admitted like I did back in 2004. I was in the hospital, left to face the circumstances that led me there, blaming others for something they didn't do instead of accepting my big role in all of it. Denial had really overtaken me. I was truly blinded by its deception. In that hospital, I had to admit that it was no one's fault but my own that I was there once more. I was beyond stressed and didn't want to face it or talk about it.

When I had the episode in 2006, I was hurt in the church because of my bipolar episodes. It was unexpected, coming from the leadership. The one place I thought wouldn't treat me differently did. Church was my safe haven; this was the house of God—His hospital—where I could go to get well spiritually, mentally, and emotionally. Instead, my spirit was broken, and my faith shattered. I stayed at that church six years longer, hoping things would get better. Ultimately, in the spring of 2012, my husband and I were given one suggestion by leadership: to leave the church.

After the episode in 2006, I threw in the towel, embraced the diagnosis, and surrendered to my doctor, counselor, and husband's counsel. My counselor asked me something that struck a nerve and made me pay attention. He said, "God made the plants that the medicine was made from. So why don't you want to take it? There's healing in the pill."

From that day forward, I began a medicinal regimen. I had tried it my way for eleven years, and it obviously wasn't working in my favor. I reflected back to my vision in April that year; it seemed like I was being set up for a comeback. After eleven years of chaos, a new beginning of God's creative work was drawing near for me to make a difference in the world.

Chapter 12

SURPRISES

THINGS WERE BACK on track for me. I had a new perspective on my life. I wasn't the same person that I was before 1995. There were changes in me beyond my control. Now that I was regularly taking my medicine, chaos had become order. My thinking had become clearer. I had a better relationship with God, although my relationship with my husband was on trial. I had to regain his trust because I had put him and my family through a lot over those eleven years.

But, surprise! I had another episode in September 2007, after my first planned family reunion in South Carolina. I felt a little unusual at the beginning of the reunion. After my remarks at the banquet, I knew I was indeed having an episode, but I didn't voice it to anyone, although my mom had her suspicions. I had gone back home to Georgia, and a few days later, my mother and second youngest sister were calling me, saying they were on the way to my house.

I thought they were just leaving Yemassee, but to my surprise, once again, they were in Villa Rica, Georgia, which was only seven miles away. I was happy they were coming to see me. I told them to hurry because I was on the way to get a dear elderly friend for a Bible study. My mom didn't think I was in any shape to go, but she and my sister got into my truck with me anyway. I went ninety miles per hour on I-20 East and looked back into the rearview mirror at my sister.

"Are you enjoying the ride?" I asked.

The look in her eyes told me I needed to slow down. So I did a little, slowing down to eighty miles per hour.

Once I got to my friend's house, she let me in her driver's seat to take us on to the Bible study. At this point, I believe we arrived at the church on a wing and a prayer. I don't remember getting there. After Bible study, we stopped by the nursing home to see my friend's sister-in-law. I gave her sister-in-law one of my sister's earrings that I had and told her, "I believe I dropped the other one in your house. So, when you find it, don't think your husband was cheating on you. It was only me there, checking on him."

A couple of days later, on Friday, September 7, 2007, I called to make an appointment with my counselor because I had noticed that I was agitated, aggravated, and fidgety; I was completely acting out of character. I had never done that before, or at least *I* never noticed, so that was certainly a new behavior in what I had called "The Year of Completion." When I got to the appointment, the doctor gave me a Haldol pill. My mom, sister, and I left the office and headed over to Sam's Club to pick up the family reunion pictures.

We started back toward my house, riding down I-20 West when I really went berserk. I was throwing pens and other things out of the window. My mom and sister called my husband to let him know they were on the way to the house, but they had to exit off the interstate because I was uncontrollable, and they weren't exactly sure what exit they had gotten off. The Haldol, my doctor, gave me had me hallucinating about the Rapture. Thankfully, my sister had locked the truck doors, because at that point my mind was telling me to get out and run! After giving my husband details of our surroundings, he was able to meet us at the convenience store where we parked.

My husband called the doctor's office, and my doctor had told him to take me to the hospital to get a shot in hopes that I would go to sleep and get some much-needed rest. After I received the shot, we sat in the hospital lobby for about fifteen minutes to see if I would have an allergic reaction. I didn't, so they took me home. I was so groggy from the medicine that I went to sleep shortly after getting to the house. I remember wanting to eat the beef stew my mom was cooking before I went to sleep. When it wasn't ready, I became extremely aggravated. Also, when I overheard them saying I needed to go to the hospital, it really sent me over the top.

I had had no intentions of ever going back to the hospital because I was complying with the doctors' orders. I was confused about how this was happening when I was faithfully taking my daily medicine like I was supposed to! All I could think about was that I had let my husband and family down again.

My family was forced to call 911 to get help for me. When the EMTs and police officers arrived, I was in my bedroom talking to my husband. They knocked on the door, and when it opened, I somehow crawled past them in that small space and ran to the kitchen, where I collided into the refrigerator. When I came to, I was lying down behind the love seat in the living room with my sister straddling me.

My sister told the officers, "No, you will not handcuff her. Lexsis, you better calm down, or they will put cuffs on you."

So, for that moment, I was calm while they placed me on the gurney and took me into the back of the ambulance. I got to the first hospital, and I was totally out of it. It was evident to me that I was saying things that were clearly not making any sense. I couldn't stop doing it as much as I wanted to.

The doctors knew I needed to be admitted, but that hospital didn't have a mental health unit. So, I was transported fifteen miles away to the hospital's affiliate. I was admitted and knew I had to be, but I also didn't think it was right for me to be there. My thoughts and speech were so irrational and inconsistent.

The next morning, I wrote a note that I wanted to be discharged. I had my way and was released from Tanner Medical Hospital, but not home to my family.

I was surprised a third time! I found myself being escorted to a patrol car by an officer who informed me that I was being transported to Anchor Hospital in Atlanta, Georgia.

I calmly replied, "This has to be a mistake because I told the nurse I wanted to be released to my husband."

The officer said, "No, it is no mistake," and he opened the backdoor of his car. He asked me, "Will you get in, please?"

I did as he requested without incident. This officer wasn't anything like the officer I had encountered years previously. He was friendly and soft-spoken. He didn't even handcuff me. He drove down I-20 East and answered every question I asked nicely.

When I was settled into my room at Anchor, my roommate came in. She was a kind lady, one whom God knew I needed to be with because she, too, was a Christian. She led us in hymns in our spare time from group sessions. When we weren't singing, we were reading Proverbs. I stuck with her most of the time I was there. I even followed her and the others on smoke breaks until one sweet day when I realized there was a non-smokers area. Whew, what a relief that was from all the cigarette smoke!

On day five of my stay there, I went in to see the doctor again, and he asked how I was feeling that day. I told him ninety-five percent myself and five percent bipolar. I thought he understood that I was joking like I did with my regular counselor, but he didn't take it as such, and I bought myself a couple more days in the hospital. So, maybe I was a little more bipolar than I thought, for thinking he could read my mind. I could have kicked myself at that point because he didn't know me well enough to know that I was joking.

He explained that I had that episode because my dosage wasn't high enough. The doctor switched the brand I was taking previously because he said it had my blood sugar level too high. After having to stay an extra two unnecessary days because of a bad joke, I was discharged to go home. I began my daily medicinal regimen and did it faithfully, but I noticed that it was making me so drowsy that it was difficult to watch after my four-year-old son.

I told my family medical physician about it, and he took a chance on me and lowered the dosage when I went for my follow-up visit. He was stern about me being compliant, and if the lower dosage didn't work, he would increase it back to where it was. I can proudly say that my physician **never** had to increase my dosage.

Nearly a year later, my relationship with my husband was being revived. After observing my consistency to be entirely recovered, he began to trust me again. I was so thankful he stuck by me those long, twelve years because he could have easily left me and taken the children. I thanked God that he had taken his vows seriously when he stood at the altar in 1998 and said, "In sickness and in health." It was very humbling. I knew that not many men would have endured the storm like he did with me. I am forever grateful that I didn't have to do it alone!

Almost twenty-six years from the first episode, and fourteen years from the last episode, I can finally testify comfortably about it. Because of that, you are able to read about my experiences: the episodes of my life.

The Encouragement

Chapter 13

SPIRITUAL DEHYDRATION

IN THE EPISODES of my life, I have been through three stages of spiritual dehydration: mild, moderate, and severe. They are like the physical dehydration stages when you go through nausea, vomiting, to having to be hooked to an IV. At different intervals of my episodes, I went through them all. They weren't necessarily progressive from one stage to the next because severe spiritual dehydration (IV fluids) occurred during the first and sixth episodes at basic training and when I was hurt by church leadership, respectively. I wasn't saved when the first one happened; the sixth time it happened, I was blindsided.

In hindsight, it scared me that I was going through this without God on my side or in my heart. When I saw the light-silhouette of Jesus, I made a conscious decision to seek God; I surrendered my life to Him a year later. God knew He had to show Himself to me at boot camp and hook me up to

His IV fluids of grace and mercy because I was really taking a chance with my eternal life.

The sixth time, I was dealing with so much stress, especially from my marital relationship and the hurt from church leadership. I wanted to quit on God even though it was sincerely my fault that the episodes occurred in the first place. I never should have written what I wanted to happen in basic training. In retrospect, knowing what I know now, I invited that "bipolar" demon into my life. I had waged spiritual warfare against myself because, at the time, I didn't realize how powerful my words were. Thankfully, the Lord hooked me up to His IV fluids again to sustain my physical and spiritual life so that I could help others. He knew I loved Him deep in my heart and had genuine compassion for His people. Deep down inside, I didn't really want to quit on God. I wanted the confusion and the pain to cease.

For example, the mild stages of spiritual dehydration (nausea) occurred when I visited my brother; and narrowly escaped being admitted. That was one of the times God brought me back to myself enough to read His Word for strength.

In the moderate cases (vomiting), when I rejected medicines, God brought two more men of God, the counselor and medical physician, into my life to allow me to see that something was going on. These two men came alongside my husband to help me and didn't stop until I got the proper treatment. They saw me first and not the illness, whereas others saw the illness first and couldn't get past it.

My spirit was resuscitated when I finally accepted their help and allowed God to strengthen me. My relationship with God began to flourish again. When the church's leadership suggested that my husband and I leave the fellowship -- at that time, I hadn't had an episode in five years -- it was only appropriate to heed it because the leadership couldn't see me as a person anymore, but only as a diagnosis. God was trying to get me to trust His process and to get me where I am today.

The only way to come out of spiritual dehydration is to allow God to revitalize you through His Word and the people He sends, good or bad. You must comply with the "medicinal regimen" that God prescribes!

Chapter 14

Yes, You Can

THERE WILL BE people who will tell you, "You can't," "You're crazy," "You're not good enough to _____," etc. But, at the end of the day, it's up to you whether or not you allow others to tell you who you are and what you are capable of because you are bipolar. Or, you can believe what God says about you over what man says. Firstly, you must realize your full potential. Secondly, while you're going through the bipolar episodes, God will speak to you, but you must listen for Him and to Him. Once you know it's Him speaking, you must act on His words.

God gave me this book title in 2005, but I was obviously not ready because it would be two episodes later before I figured out two things. One, He could heal *miraculously*, and two, He could heal *medicinally*. He chose medicinal healing for me. No, some of us who have been diagnosed as bipolar don't want to take medicine because of outsiders' labels, but it really is there to help us be able to make clearer decisions. Everyone doesn't have to know you're taking medicine for mental illness, just as you don't know the medication others take for heart disease, cancer, high cholesterol, etc. One thing is for sure: if you *don't* take your meds, others will know you are mentally ill and won't get help.

The medicine helps us live lives that allow us to make rational decisions and behave consistently with our real characters. I'd be the first to say that I made bad decisions by not complying with taking my medicine as prescribed. I certainly did not act like the person some had known by regressing to childhood at times or talking nonsense, which cost me some relationships during and long after the episodes.

You can't consider the people you will lose or have lost because they aren't supposed to make it to your future. When you can come to those terms, God can point you toward those who won't have a problem knowing that you have been diagnosed with bipolar disorder. Everybody you meet is there to teach you a lesson about who you truly are. I certainly understand that the ones I left behind taught me that they don't have the final say-so about my ability to do the things God has purposed me to do. One of those things for me was writing this book.

I was in denial for a very long time that I had a mental illness. It took me twelve long years to realize that denial wasn't helping me but was destroying me and my relationship with my husband. I hope it doesn't take you twelve years to learn the lessons of getting help and heeding it. Those are a lot of years to lose, and I wouldn't take them back because I did learn from the seven episodes I had. I'm a better and more productive person because of them.

There will be periods where it feels like you crumble under stress, pressure, or whatever sends you over the edge. But you must keep looking toward God first and the helpful people He has provided to give you sound advice. However, you must also accept that what is going on with you is real. It won't go away by ignoring it or denying it, or saying, "Name it, claim it." I don't know who came up with that phrase, but I said it, and nothing happened the way I thought it should. I was resisting the pill because I was "naming and claiming" that I was healed miraculously. However, God's healing was in the pill all the time.

What I was doing certainly wasn't faith-based because I was doing nothing. Faith requires action, not just lip service. Believe you are healed. See yourself as healed. Go to the doctor to be evaluated and follow doctors' orders. Comply with prescriptions, your follow-up visits, counseling, etc. Rest in the Lord and have patience that He will bring order to your chaos!

Once you've stabilized yourself, know that you can live a productive life; yes, you can have your own business; yes, you can be an inspiration; and yes, you can do the impossible in Christ Jesus, who gives you the strength. The choice is yours whether or not you want to be one of the labels that society puts on you or the one God has called you to. You are a part of a chosen generation, a royal priesthood, a holy nation (1 Pet. 2:9).

Here's more encouragement I'll share with you that God had to say to me, and I hope it will encourage you as well. In 2013, I decided to fast from Facebook for three days so that I could have close communication with my Heavenly Father. He sent me into the Old Testament to Joshua 1:9. It reads, "Have I not commanded you? Be strong and of good courage; do not be afraid, nor be dismayed, for the Lord your God is with you wherever you go." I was afraid of failure, but I've come to realize that when you attempt to do something good, failure is a setup for a victorious comeback.

God reminded me in Isaiah 40: 29-31 that,

> He gives power to the weak, and to those who have no might He increases strength. Even the youths shall faint and be weary, and the young men shall utterly fall, but those who wait on the Lord shall renew their strength; they shall mount up with wings like eagles, they shall run and not be weary, they shall walk and not faint.

I wanted to give up many times writing this book because I lacked confidence, but God gave me the strength to do it. I've shared some memories that were very painful to relive.

God also directed my attention to Isaiah 55: 10-11, which reads,

> For as the rain comes down, and the snow from heaven, and do not return there, but water the earth, and make it bring forth and bud, that it may give seed to the sower and bread to the eater, so shall My word be that goes forth from

> My mouth; it shall not return to Me void, but it shall accomplish what I please, and it shall prosper in the thing for which I sent it.

I knew God told me to write, but I kept making excuses for why I couldn't. His Word doesn't lie because what He had said to me all those years ago has come to fruition.

Most importantly, He said in 3 John 2, "Beloved, I pray that you may prosper in all things and be in health, just as your soul prospers." I have a home, children, a wonderful husband, my health, and sanity.

In some ways, I was afraid to move forward with this book, but I knew He had placed it on my heart to do so. I had to rely on His strength to guide me through this process. Once I started writing, I saw Joshua 1:9 in different places, such as in businesses. I even saw it along with other scriptures He'd given me on Facebook after the fast. That was when it was apparent that I was doing the right thing.

I found out too that when you humble yourself unto the Lord and leave your worries with Him, He will exalt you. Here's how 1 Peter 5: 6-11 says it:

> Therefore humble yourselves under the mighty hand of God, that He may exalt you in due time, casting all your care upon Him, for He cares for you. Be sober, be vigilant; because you adversary the devil walks about like a roaring lion, seeking whom he may devour. Resist him,

steadfast in the faith, knowing that the same sufferings are experienced by your brotherhood in the world. But may the God of all grace, who called us to His eternal glory by Christ Jesus, after you have suffered a while, perfect, establish, strengthen, and settle you. To Him be the glory and the dominion forever and ever. Amen

Hear me clearly: don't seek exaltation because that's vain. Humility is what you are seeking. Being humble will make you stronger than you could ever imagine. Keep God first, and He will deliver you from your bipolar episodes.

It was there in black and white that God wanted me to be in good health, so there was no turning back on what He had and has for me to do. No one had to tell me anymore that God wanted me healthy because He had said so to me in 3 John 2. He wants me to prosper in all things as my soul prospers.

Not only does He want this for me, but for you as well. Read the Scriptures and let them speak to your heart! You will see that I'm not making this up. God cares about your well-being too. When you have read the Word of God and accepted it in your heart, you can no longer sit around feeling sorry for yourself or blaming others. Get up from that dead party and plan a much livelier one. Christ wants us to have an abundant life! You can't start living it until you live for Him. Remain humble while you do it, and you will be exalted in due time. In Matthew 23:12, the words of Jesus say, "And whoever exalts himself will be humbled, and he who humbles himself will be exalted."

The Exaltation

Chapter 15

GLORY BELONGS TO HIM

I GIVE GOD all the glory and praise Him for being so patient with me. I thank Him for giving me such an outstanding support system, from my family and friends to my doctors and pastors. This may sound cliché, but nothing I do would be possible without God. Things I thought were impossible, such as this book, became possible. This book is now in your hands to read because I committed my ways to Him, trusted Him, and He brought them to pass. (Ps. 37:5.)

All throughout my despair, God was with me, speaking to me and through me. When He spoke, it didn't all make sense to me while I was in a manic state because there were too many racing thoughts going through my mind to comprehend. However, He gave me the ability to write during those times so that I would have a reference point when I regrouped. Sometimes I had to decipher the meaningful things and get past the ones that didn't make sense.

God is the **only** One who can ultimately help you, but you **must** be willing to surrender your plans to Him. You can't blame Him for your situation like the devil wants you to. Remember, God sent the Comforter, the Holy Spirit, to help you, not hurt you. The only way to experience God on this level is to be born again. Here's how it's done simply in Romans 10:9-10:

> That if you confess with your mouth the Lord Jesus and believe in your heart that God has raised Him from the dead, you will be saved. For with the heart one believes unto righteousness, and with the mouth confession is made unto salvation.

I don't know what would have become of me if I had not given my life to Christ. The relationship with Him surpasses human understanding. Since being submissive to Him and His will for me, the things God has done in my life have blown my mind!

I exalt God the Father, God the Son, and God the Holy Spirit above everything. After years of chaos and finally getting tired, I am here today as one of the young and the rested.

About the Author

Alexsis Boles is a child of God, wife, mother, and Sunday school teacher. She is a native of Yemassee, South Carolina, who now resides in Georgia with her husband, Reggie, and their children, Javin and Rj.

CPSIA information can be obtained
at www.ICGtesting.com
Printed in the USA
JSHW021723090622
26816JS00002B/102